Matt and Beth's powerful anthem "Blessed Be Your Name" is a gift to the Church; it has given us faith-filled words to declare when life seems to have crumbled around us. But Matt and Beth wouldn't have been able to write this song without enduring their own pain. In this book, they describe some of what they've suffered, and they share Scriptures that God used to console them. What a compassionate and mighty God we serve!

## Darlene Zschech
Songwriter and Worship Leader, Hillsong Church
Sydney, Australia
Author, *Extravagant Worship* and *Kiss of Heaven*

# BLESSED BE YOUR NAME

## MATT+BETH REDMAN

Hodder & Stoughton
LONDON SYDNEY AUCKLAND

British Library Cataloguing in Publication Data
A record for this book is available from the British Library

ISBN 0 340 90913 7

Offset by Avon DataSet Ltd, Bidford on Avon, Warwickshire
Printed and bound in Great Britain by
Clays Ltd, St Ives plc

The paper used in this hardback is a natural recyclable
product made from wood grown in sustainable forests.
The hard coverboard is recyclable.

Hodder & Stoughton
A Division of Hodder Headline Ltd
338 Euston Road
London NW1 3BH

www.madaboutbooks.com
and www.hodderbibles.co.uk

DEDICATED IN LOVING MEMORY

OF RACHEL MCCOLL AND

NATALIE KATHRYN BROWN

Rachel

Natalie

# Contents

# Foreword

The phone went at 5.00 a.m. Two dear friends were on the line. Their four-year-old was dying of a brain tumour and had been taken into hospital – would I come and pray? For the next couple of hours I just stood silently in the corner of the hospital room pleading with God as two remarkable people tried to come to terms with every parent's worst nightmare, comforting their young son in his last days.

At around 7.00 a.m. I got another call. This time it was another church member who was terminally ill with cancer and had been rushed into hospital that morning having had a massive seizure. I went down to see her in the accident and emergency ward and after she regained consciousness we started chatting together. Sarah was a woman of great faith who knew she was dying. We talked of our Christian hope of a new heaven and new earth and agreed that one day we would like to "do" the coast of Donegal together! I treasure the memory of how keen she was to know whether I thought there would be Guinness available! She was still smiling when the hospice staff arrived to take her into their care.

All the while, though, I was anxious to make two phone calls of my own. The first was to Simon. The day before he had technically died four times before being resuscitated and that morning he was having life-saving heart surgery in Brighton. I wanted to pray with him before he went down to theatre. I only just caught him in time.

The second call was to my grandmother who was in hospital and very unwell. I really wanted to get to see her but it was three hours' drive and I needed to explain why it was not going to be possible that day.

Eventually at about 10 a.m. I got in the car and tried to go into the office. I didn't make it. I felt overwhelmed, and emotionally exhausted. There was no way I was going to be able to concentrate so I went to the beach, sat on the shore and watched the waves come in.

Over the next three months I was to bury three of those four people. Over the next three months I was to sit on that beach many times.

What Matt and Beth have done in this beautiful book is to provide simple yet profound advice to help prepare Christians for those "beach moments". *Blessed Be Your Name* provides the reader with the tools for lament – how to mourn in the presence of God. This book is, in effect, a framework of Christian thinking to help us filter and view life's pain. Of course nothing can prepare us fully for suffering, quick-fix remedies do not work and, I am glad to say, are not found in these pages. What is sensitively written here points us toward a God who longs to reveal Himself in the worst of circumstances. A God who continues to bring victory in the face of death. A God who can still bring beauty out of the most awful and ugly things. A God in whom hope springs eternal.

Richard Wurmbrand who himself was imprisoned and tortured for his faith tried to explain it this way. "In prison we had to unlearn our theology and relearn *Theos* – God – the one of whom theology speaks. Nowhere in the Bible does it say that a Bible verse will comfort you. It's the living God of whom the Bible verse speaks who can only bring comfort in our suffering."

It is this God that this book encourages us to meet in our pain. Blessed be His Name!

Andy Hickford

# Blessed Be Your Name

Blessed be Your name in the land that is plentiful,
Where Your streams of abundance flow,
Blessed be Your name.
And blessed be Your name when I'm found in the desert place,
Though I walk through the wilderness,
Blessed be Your name.

Every blessing You pour out I'll turn back to praise.
And when the darkness closes in, Lord,
Still I will say,

Blessed be the name of the Lord,
Blessed be Your name.
Blessed be the name of the Lord,
Blessed be Your glorious name.

Blessed be Your name when the sun's shining down on me,
When the world's "all as it should be,"
Blessed be Your name.

And blessed be Your name on the road marked with suffering,
Though there's pain in the offering,
Blessed be Your name.

Every blessing You pour out I'll turn back to praise,
And when the darkness closes in, Lord,
Still I will say,

Blessed be the name of the Lord,
Blessed be Your name.
Blessed be the name of the Lord,
Blessed be Your glorious name.

You give and take away,
You give and take away,
My heart will choose to say,
"Lord, blessed be Your name."

# Introduction

A few years ago, while on sabbatical, we found ourselves writing a little song called "Blessed Be Your Name." Wrapped around the themes of worship, suffering and the sovereignty of God, the song was born out of a deep conviction that, come pain or joy, to worship God is always the best decision to make. The song was the soundtrack to so much of our journey in God—fatherless times when He proved to be ever faithful, and seasons of rejection and abuse when God proved to be closer than we ever knew He was. By the grace of God, we'd seen enough to trust Him—no matter how dark things appeared to be.

And trust gave birth to worship.

Since writing the song, we've heard so many stories of how the people of God have responded to Him in trust and praise—in some of the harshest life circumstances that we've ever come across. Letters, conversations and e-mails have unveiled many different tales of abuse, rejection and heartache—or stories of those who've lost loved ones in the most shocking of circumstances. Yet there's a common theme linking all of these reports together—a determined choice to press on with lives of praise amidst a world of pain. All of these worshippers have found themselves surrounded by the storms of life, and yet they have decided to respond to Jesus with a faithful cry of "Blessed be Your name" in their hearts. Come rain or shine, come hardship or ease, come confusion or clarity, they are an army of worshippers making the daily choice to respond to God with an unshakable devotion. This book is for all those who long to be counted alongside this inspiring group of worshippers.

GOD REMAINS AS

FAITHFUL AS THE DAY HE

CREATED YOU IN LOVE,

AND AS POWERFUL AS

THE DAY HE SPOKE THE

WORLD INTO BEING.

## CHAPTER ONE

# My Heart Will Choose to Say

Worship is always a choice. At times it's an easy, straightforward one. When life is peaceful and pain-less, the choice to respond to God in thanksgiving and praise may not be such a hard one to make. But at other times in our lives, worship becomes a much gutsier decision. Caught up amidst a whirlwind of pain and confusion, the decision to cry out, "Yet I will praise You," is a costly act of devotion. In the life of every worshipper there will come times when wor-ship meets with suffering. And these moments shape what kind of worshippers we will become. Yes, praise be to God for times of abundance and plenty in our lives—those carefree days full of peace and laughter. Yet we praise Him also in the wilderness times—those dark and stormy seasons of the soul when we're left crying out with the psalmist, "How long, O LORD, how long?" (Psalm 6:3).

When trials come, trust must arise. When there's nothing to rock the boat, our trust in God is rarely tested. Seasons of stillness and calm are wonderful; yet before too long the winds will start to gather, and we'll find ourselves caught up once again in the storms of life. The question then is this: Can we still find our way to the place of praise? We may have faith to believe in God as Lord of the *calm*—but do we also have faith to believe in Him as Lord of the *storm*? He is Lord of both the hurricane and the gentle breeze. The One who rules and reigns amidst all of the earthquakes of this life—those times when our whole world seems to be shaking and breaking apart.

For both of us, growing up was not an easy journey. Our childhood and teenage years were marked by family breakup and loss. Looking back now, our little stories are a testimony to the rescuing and restoring nature of God.

# Matt

For the first seven years of my life I was a carefree and contented little boy. All that changed one night in March 1981, when my dad died suddenly. It was a shocking time, and looking back now I can still picture the moment I was told of his death. A few years later I found out that he'd actually committed suicide—which came as a bit of an aftershock, and brought with it some more painful questions. Was it anything to do with me? Did he not love us enough to stay around? But by the grace of God, this painful season propelled me towards Him, and not away from Him.

A year or two later my mum (herself a passionate follower of Christ) remarried—and at first it felt like I had a new father. However, a couple of years in, things turned sour, and we soon discovered that he wasn't the man of integrity and faithfulness he claimed to be. After mistreating us as a family and abusing my trust, he was forced to leave. And again we found ourselves "fatherless."

In these dark seasons of the soul, faith is either strengthened or broken. Contentment and trust build us up. Bitterness and complaint eat us up. History is full of people who chose the path of bitterness and found themselves in an even worse place than where they started. But wise worshippers know that the only healthy way ahead is to take all they know of God and turn it into trust and praise. By His grace, even in those early teenage years, I had seen enough to know that God was good—and that time would tell He was in control. Looking back now, I can see His Father heart and His sovereign hand all over that season of my life. The passage of time has demonstrated what all along I knew to be true—that God is always closer and kinder than we know; He is a father to the fatherless.

Beth also had a gruelling childhood, bullied and abused by people she should have been able to trust. The key for both of us was that we'd seen enough of Jesus to enable us to endure. And while the enemy may have tried to use those bad circumstances to contradict the goodness of God in our minds and hearts, by the grace of God, we'd encountered Him strongly enough to trust Him—even in seasons when nothing seemed to make sense.

Such times are like a case of spiritual car sickness. Motion sickness when you travel in a car is caused by your senses contradicting each other. Say, for example, you choose to read a book as you travel. The balance sensors in your ears tell you that you're moving quickly—yet your eyes report that you're not. It's a case of conflicting senses. One way to cure the sickness is to add more evidence to what you know to be correct. For example, rolling down the window and sticking your hand out of a fast-moving car into the air will help confirm to your brain that you are indeed in motion.

The same is true of the spiritual life. There may come seasons of pain when we desperately try to cling on to what we know to be true about God, and yet we are utterly confused by a hardship we're experiencing. Our knowledge of Scripture tells us that God is eternally good; yet at the same time a very tough life situation seems to be screaming the complete opposite a t us. Before long, we find ourselves in a case of spiritual motion sickness—living in the tension of what we think we know to be true, and the deep pain that seems to contradict it.

The key is to reinforce what deep down you know to be true, by adding extra revelation. Spiritually speaking, roll down the window and stick your hand out. Open the Bible and feed upon the truths of God and His faithfulness. Strengthen your understanding of His ways as you read. Find encouragement in the lives of those who chose to trust His power, grace and purpose amidst their darkest hours. Look over His track record in your own life and in the lives of those you know to love Him. See how often He has poured out the oil of kindness in times of trouble. How on many occasions He has rescued seemingly at the last possible moment—or turned around something that at the time seemed like it could never lead to fruitfulness. All of these things build faith in us. And faith will always fan the flames of worship.

The book of Lamentations gives us a great example of a worshipper who experienced pain and yet used the act of remembering as a pathway to praise. *THE MESSAGE* words it like this:

> I remember it all  . . . the feeling of hitting the bottom. But there's one other thing I remember, *and remembering, I keep a grip on hope* (3:20-21, emphasis added).

What a fantastic way to give voice to this powerful principle! The discipline of remembering helps us keep a grip on hope and find our way on the paths of praise.

In the next verses of this chapter, the writer reminds his soul that

> GOD's loyal love couldn't have run out, his merciful love couldn't have dried up. They're created new every morning (3:22-23).

Returning to the car-sickness illustration, the worshipper here is consciously rolling down the window and sticking his hand out into the air, that he might be affirmed and strengthened in what his heart, deep down, knows to be true about God.

The writer of Lamentations was not alone in his faith-building technique. The psalmists were constantly practising this discipline. In so many of the psalms, the writer recalls the story of God's faithfulness as a bridge towards worship and hope. Psalm 13, for example, begins with a desperate cry but ends with a reminder of God's track record in his life:

> How long, O LORD? Will you forget me for
>         ever?
>     How long will you hide your face from me?
> How long must I wrestle with my thoughts
>     and every day have sorrow in my heart?

> How long will my enemy triumph over
> me? (vv. 1-2).

Five urgent questions from a worshipper longing to
be free of his suffering. Yet he ends his song with the
choice to believe and trust in the powerful and merciful nature of his God:

> But I trust in your unfailing love;
> my heart rejoices in your salvation.
> I will sing to the LORD,
> for he has been good to me (vv. 5-6).

The psalmist here teaches us a beautiful truth:
*Remembering releases rejoicing.*

Throughout the ages, the people of God have
found strength in this approach. Take, for example,
the writer of the old hymn "The Solid Rock"—a song
deeply rooted in the truth of an unchangeable,
unshakable Savior:

> When darkness veils His lovely face,
> I rest on His unchanging grace.[1]

In other words, in times when we can't seem to perceive God amidst our pain, and the clouds of anxiety and fear close in on us, the way forward is to remind ourselves of what we know to be true and dependable—the unchanging grace of God.

It's a little like looking at the moon. We've all seen a full moon and, therefore, know something of its form. But we don't always witness it like this. Some nights we see a half moon; at other times just a small sliver of moon. And on some occasions we see almost nothing at all—just the faintest outline hidden by a cloudy night sky. Yet the point is this: Even when the moon is obstructed from our view, we are still convinced of its existence and true form, because of what we have seen in the past. The same is true of our walk as worshippers of Jesus. At times, painful life circumstances seem to obstruct our view of Him and His goodness. But we have seen the form of the Lord many times before—in life and in Scripture—and know Him to be as good and as kind as He ever was. Faced with challenging times, a wise worshipper looks over the form of the Lord—recalling the soul-refreshing wonders of His nature and attributes—and through this finds a way to the place of praise. Our Father in heaven has an incredible track record.

Faced with anguish and distress, the psalmist even talked to himself. To find strength and hope, he repeatedly speaks to his soul, reminding himself that there's One who can save him. Twice he cries out in Psalm 42,

> Why are you downcast, O my soul?
>     Why so disturbed within me?
> Put your hope in God,
>     for I will yet praise him,
>         my Saviour and my God (vv. 5-6,11).

If you yourself are in a season of struggle, take a minute even now to remind yourself of the God who sees your struggle. It's possible to talk your soul into a place of hope. We worship a triumphant Saviour, a victorious King. The all-powerful and all-loving God, who is faithful in all He says and gracious in all He does. The One who has never been anxious, overwhelmed or outsmarted. The God of unbroken promises. When He acts, no one can reverse it. When He speaks, His commands never return empty. The God who never wastes His words. The doors He chooses to open, no one can close; and the doors He purposes to close, no one can open. No plan of His has ever been thwarted. No one has ever outmanoeuvred Him, outlived Him or outloved Him. He remains as faithful as the day He created you in love, and as powerful as the day He spoke the world into being. And in your brokenness He stays as close and as involved as you want Him to be.

To worship God is to tell Him that we believe Him for who He says He is. Every day we're faced with the choice either to acknowledge and proclaim Him as the great and merciful God He declares Himself to be—or to deny Him. Intense though it may sound, the truth is this: If we are to deny something good about God, we automatically imply something bad about Him. If we deny God's sovereignty and power, then we imply that, to a degree at least, He is weak and has lost control. If we can't bring ourselves to trust that He is full of mercy, then perhaps, at least in part, we're implying that He has a mean or uncaring streak. There is actually no middle ground. He either is the all-powerful, all-loving God who His Word declares Him to be—or He is not.

That may sound a touch harsh—and please hear it in the context of the incredible wealth of patience, kindness and compassion stored up for us in the heart of God. For in His amazing grace, our heavenly

Father finds delight even in the most broken and fragile of our offerings—in the same way that an earthly father will rejoice upon receiving a simple yet heartfelt piece of art from his young child. Yet this is only one side of the mystery, for our God is also the majestic and holy King—worthy to be trusted and believed in for the wonderful truths of who He says He is. He desires and requires faith, trust and obedience—He wants worshippers who stake their lives on the truths of His nature and attributes.

Note the heart posture of a Nazi concentration-camp prisoner who once scribbled these lines onto the wall of his cell:

> I believe in the sun
> Even when it is not shining.
> I believe in love
> Even when I feel it not.
> I believe in God
> Even when He is silent.[2]

Yes, every act of worship is a choice—a decision to believe and respond to God for who He says He is—no matter how pressing our circumstances. And the greater the pain we're experiencing, the greater a choice it may be. Sometimes we will walk blindly, unable to understand why we are going through a certain situation—our only comfort being the knowledge that God Himself is not walking blindly, but instead is wisely, kindly and firmly in control. Indeed, as we will begin to see, so often our Father in heaven will take our broken moments and weave them into a powerful tapestry to the glory of His name.

—✺—

THE CHURCH OF GOD

NEEDS HER SONGS OF

LAMENT JUST AS MUCH

AS SHE NEEDS HER

SONGS OF VICTORY.

—✺—

## CHAPTER TWO

# The Road Marked with Suffering

On September 15, 2001, we flew into L.A. for the start of a sabbatical break in California. Four days earlier we'd watched with the rest of the world, gripped by those terrible, nation-shaking events of 9/11. Over the next few days and weeks in the U.S., as we watched the news, talked with neighbours and visited many different churches, the full effect of the terrorist attacks began to unfold before us. Brokenness was everywhere, and many people sought some kind of comfort in the Church. Our landlady, who just weeks before had relocated to Manhattan, set foot inside a church building for the first time since her childhood. For the few weeks following those attacks, church attendance figures all over America went up dramatically.

During this time we had the privilege of visiting many different congregations. We were so inspired and impressed by the preachers. Virtually everywhere we went, pastors delivered biblical and powerful sermons, speaking into the pain of the nation. They eloquently and powerfully expressed the heart of God over a shocked and vulnerable people—and reminded them of His strength and sovereignty. But nearly everywhere we visited, a worrying question began to arise: Where were the songwriters at such a time as this? Where were the musical poets and prophets to help the people of God find a voice in worship at this tragic time? The truth was, in most places we visited (or led worship in), there was a distinct lack of songs appropriate for this time. As songwriters and lead worshippers, we had a few expressions of hope at our disposal; but when it came to expressions of pain and lament, we had very little vocabulary to give voice to our heart cries. On a few occasions, we did encounter a helpful song for these vulnerable times—but for the most part, it seemed as if we and many of our fellow lead worshippers were struggling to find the right tone. The truth is, the Church of God needs her songs of lament just as much as she needs her songs of victory.

It wasn't the first time we'd noticed this gap. Once before, we'd flown into San Diego, California, for a worship conference—just a couple of days after a horrific school-shooting incident right there in the heart of the city. Since we were staying in town during one of the memorial services, we were asked to lead worship for some of the students and their families. We accepted straight away and immediately began to ponder which songs might best fit the tone of the time. David Ruis's "Whom Have I But You" was a God-send:

Though my coloured dawn
May turn to shades of grey
Whom have I but You?[1]

And the hymn "Amazing Grace"—particularly the "dangers, toils, and snares" verse—played a big part too.[2] But again we were left in a slightly vacant space—struggling to find more songs that would help the community respond to God healthily, biblically and honestly at such a time.

A few weeks after 9/11, we wrote the worship song "Blessed Be Your Name." It wasn't written consciously in response to those dark events—but no doubt, being immersed in the spiritual and emotional climate of those days was an important factor in birthing it. Many people ask if there was a particular life event that triggered off the writing of this song, and in all truth, the answer is no. It's really a song born out of the whole of life—a realization that we will all face seasons of pain or unease. And in these seasons we will need to find our voice before God. The Church (and indeed the world) needs its songs of lament.

The people of God have always had their laments. The book of Psalms is filled with a host of intense emotions and expressions toward God. So many of the psalms were birthed in times of suffering and struggle. Psalm 3 was written as King David fled for his life from his own son Absalom. Psalm 56 was inspired when the Philistines captured him in Gath. In Psalm 57 David is on the run again, this time from King Saul—and he wrote the song while hiding in a cave. These are songs formed in the fire of affliction. They are the desperate cries of a worshipper on the road marked with suffering. In fact, Eugene Peterson estimates that around 70 percent of the content of the book of Psalms is lament based.[3]

Clearly, therefore, songs of lament are a very biblical thing to sing in worship. Yet they are also a relevant thing to sing—for we live in a world full of anguish and heartache. As Christians, yes, we live in victory—but paradoxically we also exist as strangers in a foreign land, aching for home and knowing deep within us that the world we see before us is not as it should be. So the question is this: If songs of lament are, first, thoroughly biblical and, second, extremely relevant, then why on earth are there not more songs to help us voice these heart cries?

As Frederick W. Schmidt, Jr., writes, these psalms do three things:

> They give us permission to ask our own questions about suffering. They model the capacity to ask questions we might otherwise suppress, but can never escape. And they model how those questions might be asked without fear of compromising our relationship with God or with other people.[4]

Not only do these songs help us to be "real" in worship—but as Mark Greene from the London Institute for Contemporary Christianity points out, they also help us give solidarity with the pain of the world.[5]

Some people may argue that lament is not an appropriate expression for gathered worship—they ask, "How can we respond in such a tone when not everyone in the room may be feeling that way?" Again, Mark Greene is helpful, pointing out that to think like that is far too individualistic.[6] Our gathered worship is a community event—and therefore we mourn with those who mourn, and weep with those who weep. If we do not feel like lamenting on a particular occasion, then perhaps we can sing the song to identify with any in our church family (or indeed the world) who do. Maybe on another occasion they themselves will be in a brighter place and yet will sing and cry out to God in solidarity with our pain. As Paul reminded us in 1 Corinthians 12,

> If one part suffers, every part suffers with it (v. 26).

For those in pain, it's very freeing to realize that we may ask questions in worship. Jesus Himself (our

blueprint for perfect worship) did so as He suffered
the agonies of the cross. The crucified King of kings
uttered words from a psalm of lament as He hung in
agony:

> My God, my God, why have you forsaken
> me? (Psalm 22:1; Mark 15:33).

Cries for help and painful questions are well
within the bounds of healthy and biblical worship.
The psalms model that for us on so many occasions.
Yet what they also model is an underlying, worshipful
trust in their God. The cry of their writers, however
loud or long, and however dark or desperate, never
wanders into the realm of accusation. The psalmists
never suggest that perhaps God is not who He says He
is after all. And as Schmidt, Jr., notes, the writers
"strain and search for understanding and act on what
they learn. But getting answers to their questions is
not the basis of their relationship with God."[7]

Though they may be stripped of confidence, and
though they may be struggling to muster up
strength and faith, these worshippers never journey
into utter *hopelessness*. Utter weakness and despera-
tion, yes. Yet even in their most desperate of times,

there is always an undercurrent of hope—a knowing conviction that though they walk through the valley of the shadow of death, their God is everything He says He is. He is both shepherd and fortress—the God of unequalled compassion and of unrivalled strength.

God delights in such offerings—an underlying trust in His goodness and greatness, when our circumstances around us seem to fly in the face of our beliefs. Perhaps in the same way that a seed of faith is enough to move a mighty mountain, so too a seed of hope and trust is enough to move the heart of Almighty God.

Our good friend Tim Hughes wrote a powerful song that wraps itself around this theme of lament and questioning—yet is marked by an underlying sense of trust, which is never far below the surface. The searching cries of the verse allow us to be real before God—and confess in our brokenness that our lives are not as together as we would like them to be:

I've had questions, without answers,
I've known sorrow, I have known pain.

Yet next comes a brilliant flow of lyrics, reminding us of how a broken heart might move healthily onward in worship:

When hope is lost, I'll call You Saviour.
When pain surrounds, I'll call You healer.[8]

When we're feeling abandoned or hopeless, we must declare Him as Saviour. And when we're overcome by anguish and pain, we must throw ourselves at the feet of the One we know to be the healer. When our circumstances seem to dictate differently, the remedy is to confess, as urgently as possible, what deep down we know to be true about God.

It's important to note that in taking such a stand, we are not *bargaining* with God. It is not a case of "I'll scratch your back if you scratch mine"—or, in other words, "I'll call You Saviour if You agree to heal me." Instead we are proclaiming Him for who He is and then falling upon His mercy and good judgment. In His infinite wisdom and kindness, God may well purpose to bring us healing. But perhaps we will have to wait awhile to see our situation changed. Or perhaps we will never be healed this side of heaven. And if we are not, God hasn't become any less wise or merciful. Indeed, one day we may well realize for ourselves just how merciful and wise He was in withholding a healing. We are entirely in the hands of His great mercy and wisdom.

The story of Shadrach, Meshach and Abednego in the book of Daniel demonstrates this attitude powerfully. Refusing to bow down in worship before anyone but their God, these worshippers are threatened with a raging furnace—certain death in the eyes of their aggressor and all those around them. Refusing to bow the knee in the face of repeated threats, they declare,

> "If we are thrown into the blazing furnace, the God we serve is able to save us from it, and he will rescue us from your hand, O king. *But even if he does not*, we want you to know, O king, that we will not serve your gods or worship the image of gold you have set up" (3:17-18, emphasis added).

Of course, the story ends with their surviving the fire—without a hair on their head being singed and without even the smell of fire on them. But the real point here is that their attitude is a great role model for us as worshippers. In our darkest times, we must proclaim Jesus as the One who is powerful enough to heal and merciful enough to rescue. But all the time, underneath must be a conviction that even if for some reason we are not relieved of our struggle, our worship will not falter. At times, we may find ourselves faced with our own raging furnaces—be it persecution or other forms of suffering. And the principle is the same for us as it was for those friends of Daniel thousands of years ago. We rest worshipfully on a high view of the sovereignty of God and a deep knowledge of His Father heart.

At one time or another, we will all experience both sides of this situation—times when God grants our requests for healing or rescuing, and times when He chooses not to. At the time of writing, we're in the middle of a recent and still painful example of this, having just experienced a third successive miscarriage.

## Beth

When Matt and I suffered the loss of a baby again and again, I began to do what so many of us do when we're in pain—to notice how others around me were being prospered and blessed. How people who didn't even try to honour God seemed to have such fruitful lives without any hardship. I felt so dismayed and confused. It just seemed so upside down: to try to live right before God and aim to be humble and obedient, only to suffer as a consequence. Psalm 73 summed it all up for me:

> But as for me, I came so close to the edge of the cliff!
>     My feet were slipping, and I was almost gone.
> For I envied the proud
>     when I saw them prosper. . . .
> They seem to live such a painless life;
>     their bodies are so healthy and strong.
> They aren't troubled like other people
>     or plagued with problems like everyone else.
> Was it for nothing that I kept my heart pure
>     and kept myself from doing wrong?
>         (vv. 2-5,13, NLT).

To see the tiny frame of a baby's body, lifeless on a screen, with no heartbeat; and then, at an early stage of pregnancy, to have to go through a mini-labour and hand that baby back to Jesus—that was one of the hardest times in my life. Why was it happening? Then to lose two more babies in a row, even when I'd sought God so hard, was almost more than I could handle. Bitterness started to beckon, and again Psalm 73 seemed to perfectly describe my pain:

> I must have seemed like a senseless animal to you (v. 22, NLT).

In the early stages of my first miscarriage, I hid away, battling in prayer. As I was physically losing the baby, I pleaded with God, for I knew He had the power to stop it. I became like Hannah in the temple, who pleaded and wailed for the baby she longed for. I knew that, in a moment, the baby could be restored and the pregnancy could continue. Would God show mercy and favour like He did to Hannah?

But there came a moment when I knew it was all over and that the baby was lost. From that moment on, I started to relate more to the story of King David—who himself lost a child after much prayer and petition (see 2 Samuel 12). David accepted the news of the child's death as the sovereign will of God, got up from the ground and worshipped Him. There is a prayer that says, "God grant me the serenity to accept the things I cannot change," and that was the beauty of David's devotion in that moment. For there is a time to wail and weep, plead, shout and grieve. But there is a time to accept the situation, get up off the floor and somehow try to worship.

After our second miscarriage, I grieved harder and realized that the longing for a baby was all I could talk to God about. It almost had become an idol—with my desire for a baby starting to supersede my need and longing for God. I soon felt convicted—and once again found solace in the words of Psalm 73:

> Yet I still belong to you;
>> you are holding my right hand.
> You will keep on guiding me with your counsel,
>> leading me to a glorious destiny.
> Whom have I in heaven but you?
>> I desire you more than anything on earth.
> My health may fail, and my spirit may grow weak,
>> but God remains the strength of my heart;
>> he is mine forever (vv. 23-26, NLT).

By His grace I saw things in a new light—that even if I never had another baby, God had already given me everything I need in Christ Jesus.

Soon after our third miscarriage, we felt challenged with the words of 1 Thessalonians 5:16:

> Be joyful always; pray continually; give thanks in all circumstances, for this is God's will for you in Christ Jesus.

In the midst of this turmoil it is right to grieve, and it is healthy to express our pain to God. But is also God's will for us in Christ to be joyful, prayerful and thankful in every circumstance. At times that is almost too hard for us—but if we can get hold of it, the deep and freeing truth is that if we're in Christ Jesus, we can never be completely joyless. As the apostle Paul described it, "Sorrowful, yet always rejoicing" (2 Corinthians 6:10). Yes, I still grieve—but in the depths of my heart I know that God Himself is more than I need. And I know too that if it's His will for us to hold another baby in our arms, then no closed womb, no condition doctors cannot explain, no age barrier or genetic condition could ever hold back His plan.

A few years ago we discovered an old hymn by
Laurence Tuttiett—a beautiful expression by a worshipper who had decided that come what may, he
was determined to live for the glory of God:

> Father, let me dedicate all this [life] to thee,
> In whatever worldly state thou would have
>     me be.
> Not from sorrow, pain or care freedom dare
>     I claim,
> This alone shall be my prayer, glorify thy
>     Name.

It's a costly song to sing—for without a deep belief in
God's sovereign wisdom and strength, and in His
merciful and kind Father heart, it's far too risky a
lyric to utter. The hymn continues along the same
theme:

> Can a child presume to choose where or
>     how to live?
> Can a Father's love refuse all the best to
>     give? . . .
> Let my glad heart, while it sings, thee in all
>     proclaim,

And, whate'er the future brings, glorify thy
  Name.[9]

This is a weighty offering of worship—standing
before God, vowing to choose Him above the circumstances of this life, to love and follow Him come
what may. But those who do so are never left disap-
pointed. For you cannot outgive God.

There will no doubt be many things in this splin-
tered world that we will not understand this side of
heaven. And we simply take assurance in the fact that
God is all we have, but more than we need. As John
Piper writes,

There are seasons of pain and loss and grief
and darkness when nothing else is worth
asking for but God.[10]

So often, the soil

of our suffering will

become the fertile

ground for our

seasons of

fruitfulness.

## CHAPTER THREE

# Though There's Pain in the Offering

There's no doubt about it: This world is a harsh place to live. Every day over 2,000 people end their lives in suicide.[1] And no one goes through this world untouched by tragedy. All around us are people struggling to come to terms with suffering—so many stories of depression, rejection, terminal illness, miscarriage, bereavement and many other hardships. On a wider scale, the picture can seem even bleaker. A daily glance at the evening news reminds us of what a harsh place we inhabit. Hardly a day goes by without a major tragedy hitting our screens. Floods and earthquakes, suicide bombers, train wrecks, paedophile networks, wars and famines, cancer scares—the list is seemingly endless.

Statistics provide us with yet more evidence of a broken world. In sub-Saharan Africa alone, some 25.4 million people are infected with HIV; and in the year 2004 alone, an estimated 2.3 million people in that region died of full-blown AIDS. In fact, in nine African countries, life expectancy at birth has now dropped below 40 years of age.[2]

If we're not careful, these news stories and statistics soon become just a list of facts and figures. But these reports are about real people—individuals struggling to retain the will to live as they carry their heavy burdens along the road of suffering. And the God of heaven, who has compassion on all that He has made, is weeping with them.

Wholesome worship never minimizes the pain of this world. It could be all too easy to sing our victorious songs, forever sweeping the hardships of this life under the carpet. A far healthier approach is to acknowledge before God the pain of this life, and then choose Him in the midst of it—not trying to deny or somehow superficially rise above our pain, but instead welcoming Him right into the reality of the situation. For some of us, worship will demand a gritty perseverance, by which we decide daily to choose the worth and ways of God over and above the pain of the struggle.

Yet wholesome worship, though not disregarding pain, does not disregard joy either. Even in the midst of deep pain, there is always an undercurrent of hope. For if we live in Christ, we can never be completely joyless. Yes, we must be honest and real in our struggles (as we've affirmed, lament is actively modelled in Scripture). But we must not sink down into the pits of despair and give up the fight, disregarding everything we know of God and disengaging with His merciful nature and goodness. If we do so, then we have lost our distinctive as followers of Christ, and our songs become no different from the despairing dirges of the culture around us—some of which start in pain, end in pain, and never have a hope of journeying anywhere else.

The Christian distinctive not only accepts pain as a fact of life but also even learns to be thankful in it:

Give thanks in all circumstances, for this is
God's will for you in Christ Jesus (1 Thessalonians 5:18).

Though clearly we would never celebrate pain for
pain's sake, from the canvas of Scripture and from
the tapestry of our own lives, we begin to recognize
that in times of anguish God is always closer and
more at work than we know. Though there is pain in
the offering, we cry out, "Blessed be Your name"—
and before long, we often begin to witness the fruit
of all He has accomplished in us or through us during these seasons of struggle. The writer of James
expressed it like this:

Consider it pure joy . . . whenever you face
trials of many kinds, because you know that
the testing of your faith develops perseverance. Perseverance must finish its work so
that you may be mature and complete, not
lacking anything (James 1:2-4).

Journey through the New Testament and we dis-
cover that time and time again the writers of these
letters reinforce the same thread of teaching. First

Peter 1:7 tells us that our temporary trials have come so that our faith "may be proved genuine and may result in praise, glory and honour when Jesus Christ is revealed." The apostle Paul did not unwillingly endure hardships, but for the sake of Christ, delighted in them—for he knew a deep truth:

> When I am weak, then I am strong (2 Corinthians 12:10).

The book of Hebrews encourages us to see hardship as discipline—reasoning that it's all part of being a child of God:

> Endure hardship as discipline; God is treating you as sons. For what son is not disciplined by his father? If you are not disciplined (and everyone undergoes discipline), then you are illegitimate children and not true sons (12:7-8).

The writer continues on:

> Our fathers disciplined us for a while as they thought best; but God disciplines us for our

good, that we may share in his holiness. No
discipline seems pleasant at the time, but
painful. Later on, however, it produces a harvest of righteousness and peace for those
who have been trained by it (12:10-11).

These two verses are vital to our understanding of this
whole process in God. The writer makes it clear that
it's not a case of masochism; in other words, we don't
enjoy being in pain. No discipline seems pleasant at
the time. In our hearts, minds or bodies, we may be
struggling beneath the pain of a testing situation. But
deep in our spirits, we learn to consider it joy, knowing
that we not only can find Christ in the situation but
also can become more like Him as a result of it. There
are no wasted seasons in the economy of God.

In *THE MESSAGE*, Eugene Peterson phrases this
Hebrews passage beautifully, throwing yet more light
on the essence of the passage:

My dear child, don't shrug off God's discipline,
     but don't be crushed by it either.
It's the child he loves that he disciplines;
     the child he embraces, he also corrects
     (12:5-6).

As C. S. Lewis once wrote,

> God whispers to us in our pleasures, speaks
> in our conscience, but shouts in our pains—
> it is his megaphone to rouse a deaf world.[3]

The more we journey through these New Testament letters, the more we recognize just how prominent this thread of teaching is. In 2 Corinthians 1:8-9, Paul recognizes that he suffered so that he might become more dependent on God. And the apostle Peter tells his readers that grief and trials have come so that their faith can be proved genuine and can result in "praise, glory and honour" (1 Peter 1:7).

Hebrews 2:10 tells us that Jesus Himself was made "perfect through suffering." Or as the *New Living Translation* expresses it, "Through the suffering of Jesus, God made him a perfect leader, one fit to bring them into their salvation." To see this throws a whole new light on our thinking about the trials of this life. If we are seeking to be followers of Jesus, sharpened and matured in our faith, can we really expect to escape times of suffering, when the Author and Perfecter of our faith embraced and endured them?

This area is in many ways a hard teaching, and if it wasn't in the Bible in such clear and blunt language, we might even find it hard to swallow. The truth is, so often when we perceive God to have left us to struggle alone, the complete opposite is in fact true—He has not left the scene, but instead is doing a deep work in us. C. S. Lewis helps us further to understand this biblical way of thinking:

> We are . . . a Divine work of art, something that God is making, and therefore something with which He will not be satisfied until it has a certain character. Over a sketch made idly to amuse a child, an artist may not take much trouble: he may be content to let it go even though it is not exactly as he meant it to be. But over the great picture of his life—the work which he loves . . . he will take endless trouble—and would, doubtless, thereby *give* endless trouble to the picture. . . . One can imagine a picture, after being rubbed and scraped and recommenced for the tenth time, wishing that it were only a thumbnail sketch whose making was over in a minute. In the same

way, it is natural for us to wish that God
had designed for us a less glorious and less
arduous destiny; but then we are wishing
not for more love but for less.[4]

What an amazing insight into this process! We are
back to Hebrews 12—that those whom our heavenly
Father loves, He disciplines. His hand may be heavy
upon us at times; yet He comes to discipline, not to
condemn. "There is now no condemnation for those
who are in Christ Jesus" (Romans 8:1).

Though the discipline may not seem pleasant at
the time, it's far easier to endure (or count as joy and
delight in!) if somehow within the bigger picture
we manage to see the brushstrokes of God. As the
seventeenth-century Madame Guyon commented,

It is the fire of suffering which will bring forth
the gold of godliness.[5]

A word of warning: We're not trying to advocate
that every kind of suffering is merely a blessing in
disguise. That could be a massively insensitive stance
to take, especially in the light of major world
tragedies, such as Auschwitz or the more recent

South Asian tsunami. Or even in the light of something far more individual and personal, such as losing a loved one. We can't simply tidy away the issue of suffering into an "every cloud has a silver lining" drawer. The issue is far more complex than that—and many times we ourselves cannot provide a satisfactory answer to the question of why suffering occurs. To always attempt an explanation may at times put us at risk of belittling someone's experience of suffering—or in danger of second-guessing Almighty God. As Frederick Schmidt, Jr., writes, "It would be arrogant or irreverent for us to claim we completely understand the mind of God."[6] Some situations are far beyond our fathoming. And whether or not we can directly trace the handiwork of God in a certain situation, we can always find comfort in the fact that He is closer than we know. God is not in the habit of leaving us stranded.

And yet, so often we do begin to see God at work even in the hardest of circumstances. The story of Joseph in the book of Genesis provides us with an inspiring example of this. Toward the end of the story, after Joseph had been beaten up by his brothers and sold into slavery, and then elevated in Pharaoh's court, only to be imprisoned unjustly once again, he explains to his repentant brothers his take on things:

> "You intended to harm me, but God intended it for good" (50:20).

Joseph goes on to explain that God used the situation to bring about the saving of many lives. We would do well to follow Joseph and adopt a heart posture that is quick to recognize the hand of the Lord working even in times of trouble. Years before this, Joseph had learned this dynamic of God's working in the midst of suffering:

> The second son [Joseph] named Ephraim and said, "It is because God has made me fruitful in the land of my suffering" (41:52).

This is a vital principle to keep hold of if we're to persevere. So often, the soil of our suffering will become the fertile ground for our seasons of fruitfulness. The sooner we recognize this principle at work in various situations, the less painful they may be. If we can see that we will reap a harvest, we will have a greater readiness to sow in tears.

We've experienced this in our lives—so many of the hardest times have led to fruitfulness in our own lives and in the Kingdom. What was meant for harm, God meant for good, bringing beauty out of ashes and making us fruitful in the land of our suffering. It's now clear to see how, during years of rejection and abuse early on in our lives, God drew us close to Himself and turned those years around to prepare us for lives of Kingdom ministry in Him.

Throughout the Bible we see this pattern time and time again. Just as God did in the life of Joseph, in His wisdom He often puts His people through a training school to prepare them for work in His Kingdom. King David is a prime example. Anointed for victory in his battle against Goliath, David soon became a national hero, and his profile accelerated rapidly. People began to sing their songs about him, and he enjoyed favour in the courts of the king, where he then lived. Humanly speaking, he may have been thinking, *Now is my time.* He knew full well that he'd been anointed as the next king—and surely that was the logical next step, wasn't it? But things soon turned sour, and God propelled him into a season of yet more character training—living in caves for seven years, while the bitter King Saul sought to kill him. In that season he must have asked what on earth was happening—it seemed as if the call on his life was slipping through his fingers. But God had other plans: He used this time in the desert as an opportunity to form in David the qualities He required for a king. David was soon to be trusted with an incredible amount of fame, fortune and power—and this season of hardship would sharpen him as the next leader of God's people. Suffering prepared him for the entrustment of kingship.

In John 15, Jesus paints a fantastic picture of how God often works in our lives. He describes the Father as a gardener, telling His disciples,

> "Every branch that does bear fruit he prunes
> so that it will be even more fruitful" (v. 2).

In the natural world, the pruning of a rose bush, for example, ensures that excess is removed, and helps to concentrate energy in the plant—getting it ready for more fruitfulness. In the same way, God gets involved in our lives, pruning even what is fruitful so that we may blossom more in our walk with Him.

# Matt

Seven years ago I experienced a very real sense of God's pruning when I developed an acute form of tendonitis in my arm. In that particular season, I was crazily busy as a lead worshipper, leading worship at church, recording an album and travelling at the same time—with little rest in between. It all came to a head one weekend when, after four days of nonstop guitar playing in the studio, I headed off to Holland for some worship gatherings. On Friday night, I started to feel a strong twinge in my strumming arm, which by Saturday had turned into an agonizing pain. By Sunday morning, I could barely move my whole arm and hand. Seeking medical advice for nearly a week and misdiagnosed on more than one occasion, I finally found a specialist, who informed me that my hand had frozen up. He then told me that if I'd come a day or two later, I would perhaps have lost full use of that hand. It was a scary moment.

I couldn't play guitar for seven weeks, and during that time many people prayed for me and sent encouraging words. Most of the words hit the mark powerfully, and their insights resonated deep within me. One or two, though, focused intensely on the phrase "the work of the enemy." Strangely, these didn't sit well with me—for by then I had a strong conviction that enemy or no enemy, what I was experiencing, more than anything else in that season, was a deep work of the Lord in me. As a lead worshipper, I'd become far too busy—and busyness had led me to neglect some of the main and plain things of the Christian walk, such as being mindful of the Lord in prayer and through His Word. This painful time was a spiritual pit stop—a chance to have some vital work done under the hood, before any lasting damage occurred. God was reminding me that the *work of the Lord* should never outweigh the *Lord of the work*— and that I was a *son* long before I was a *servant*. Stripping me of pride and self-confidence also, my Father was reminding me that His power is made perfect in weakness.

To this day I don't know exactly what was at play theologically during that time. Was it the Lord inflicting it? Or was it the Lord allowing the enemy to do so? These questions slowly faded into the background, as I rested safe in the knowledge that, whatever the case, my Father was very much in control,

disciplining me with kindness and care—in the way
that a perfect Father does.

When we look back over our lives, we can see the
Lord's marks of kindness everywhere. So often in times
of joy and celebration, all of us are quick to recognize
the hand of God. But as mature Christians, we begin to
recognize His presence in the face of adversity too—seeing God powerfully at work in our brokenness.

Recently we were out driving in the countryside,
when we suddenly realized that we were nearly out of
fuel. From that moment on, the journey changed. We
were as light on the gas pedal as possible, driving care-
fully at an optimum speed for efficiency, and staring
hopefully out of the window for the first sign of a
place to refuel. We had realized our emptiness, recog-
nizing afresh just how dependent on fuel we were—
and becoming much more thankful for every drop,
treating it as something precious.

The same dynamic happens in the life of every
worshipper. We may go through life cruising com-
fortably, taking the things of God for granted, and
therefore not as mindful of Him as we should be. It's

in these times that in God's great mercy, He shakes us up to realize our dependence on Him, and our brokenness without Him. He may strip us of something we have come to depend on outside of Him, or find another way to remind us of our poverty without Him. Before long, there's a new sense of dependence on Him, and a heightened gratitude for every single drop of His grace in our lives.

Sometimes, on this journey it may take months—even years—for the full evidence of fruitfulness to appear before our eyes. Such seasons require endurance and patience, and they challenge us to leave behind our "instant everything" mentality, which is so prominent in today's culture. When it comes to the Kingdom of God, fast-food spirituality is not on the menu. We're left instead to embrace these seasons of silence, once again leaning upon the track record of God's faithfulness, until rejoicing arrives in the morning. As Oswald Chambers both challenges and encourages us,

> Has God trusted you with a silence—a silence that is big with meaning? . . . If God has given you a silence, praise Him, He is bringing you into the great run of His purposes.[7]

There may be a time of waiting—and then all at once it becomes very evident that God has made us fruitful in the land of our suffering. Yet, as we acknowledged previously, for all of us there will be times when however hard we scrutinize the situation, however much we search for wisdom from Scripture or seek counsel from a pastor, we simply cannot begin to understand where God is in our suffering. And this will always be a much harder pill to swallow. There are situations on this earth that we may never fully make sense of while we're living here—taking comfort only in the fact that we are not alone in our suffering. God Himself is involved—weeping with those who weep and drawing near to the broken-hearted. The wonderful truth is that, however broken we feel, we have not been left alone to make our own way out of the darkness. Though we walk even through the shadow of death, we learn to recognize the closeness of Jesus—for shadows can only be caused by the presence of light.

And here and now upon the earth, the cross of Christ illuminates our way on the road marked with suffering. In the light of Calvary, where the Son of God so willingly surrendered His life for this world, we find both strength and hope for our times of need. The Cross reminds us that we worship a God who identifies with our suffering. One who is able to show both compassion and empathy, for He Himself was overwhelmed by anguish and pain. Yet the Cross also works another miracle—wherein the mercy of that place begins to outweigh the misery of our situation. Somewhere deep within we may still be asking, "Jesus, why am I suffering in this way?" But before long that question, valid as it may be, will be superseded by another one. Standing at the foot of the Cross, we begin to ask, "Jesus, how can it be that You would suffer in that way?" The answer reminds us that we are not alone in suffering; more than anything it assures us once again of the magnitude of His mercy. It is not escapism, but realism. The mercy of God outweighing the mess of our lives.

EVERY DAY GOD IS

WORKING OUT HIS

WONDERS ALL

AROUND US.

## CHAPTER FOUR

# Turn It Back to Praise

So far in the pages of this book we've looked at worshipping God on the road marked with suffering. But let's focus for one chapter on the other side of things—making sure that we journey to the place of praise in times of abundance. The fact is, we can be quick to question God when things go wrong for us, but slow to honour Him when things go well. The challenge is to take every blessing He pours out on our lives, and turn it back into praise. As someone once commented, "Saying thank you is more than good manners. It is good spirituality."[1]

Gratitude is an essential ingredient in our worship "diet." Indeed, thanksgiving has always been a great way for the people of God to take a first step into worship. As Psalm 100 exhorts us,

> Enter his gates with thanksgiving
>     and his courts with praise;
>         give thanks to him and praise his name
>             (vv. 4-5).

Gratitude is a heart attitude that we must train ourselves in—for we're so quick to neglect it. Scanning through Scripture, time and again we see the people of God needing some direction in this area. The story of the Exodus and the people of God wandering discontentedly around the desert show just how easy it is for murmuring and moaning to set in—leading us far from the paths of gratitude and contentment. And on many occasions, the likes of the psalms and the New Testament letters remind us to be thankful—highlighting yet again that this may not always be the first instinct of our hearts. The story of the 10 lepers illuminates this even further. Jesus healed all 10, but only 1 returned to Him in thanks and praise (see Luke 17:11-37). Where were the other 9? For some reason, they just kept on walking. Perhaps they had meant to return in thanksgiving at some point, but became distracted with celebrating and never quite got round to it. Perhaps they got too wrapped up in themselves and forgot the One who was the source of their joy and healing. Yet it's easy to see ourselves in this picture—so often receiving the gift but somehow, in the midst of the blessing, forgetting the Giver. Our consumer-driven society has birthed a generation of takers. We'd do well to be led in worship by that one returning leper—who praised God loudly and threw himself at the feet of Jesus in extravagant thanksgiving.

The discipline of thanksgiving involves a constant stream of decisions to recognize and respond to the many kindnesses that have been poured out on us. The more we cultivate this heart posture, the more it will begin to flow naturally in our lives. It's like a small snowball at the top of a hill. Choose to set it in motion, guiding it down the slope, and it soon grows larger and larger. At a certain point, it runs away with itself, developing a momentum all of its own. In the same way, when we become mindful of thanking God for even the smallest details of our lives, we soon find ourselves caught up in an endless list of things to be grateful for.

We need look no further than our bodies to get the ball rolling. The biology of our bodies has to be one of the most overlooked things when it comes to prayers of gratitude towards God. Do you like your own body? You should. We are an incredible mix of cells—with organs of such mind-blowing complexity that the best man-made technologies of our day still come no way near to matching them. So many of the complex internal parts we use every day, we barely give a second thought to. But when we take a moment to marvel at them, they become a fantastic opportunity to explode in thankfulness before God.

Take the brain, for example. When was the last time you thanked God for your brain? That you can remember names, faces and life events? That you can read the pages of His Word and store Scripture verses in your mind? That you can compute, conceive and store in your memory so many of the wonders He has made? With 500,000 kilometres of nerve fibres and messages travelling along them at speeds of a hurricane-force wind, the brain is something to be incredibly thankful for.[2] Yet it is just one part of our fantastically designed anatomy.

When was the last time you went to God in gratitude for your heart? The human heart beats 100,000 times a day and, in the space of 70 years, would pump enough blood to fill a skyscraper. The volume of blood pumped each minute is about 5 litres. But during physical exertion, the volume per minute can rise to 25 litres—so that the entire blood volume is pumped through the body five times per minute.[3] You'll never give thanks with a grateful *heart* in the same way again!

Move on to your senses—have you ever wondered that you can smell your favourite flower, taste your favourite food, and hear all kinds of interesting and moving music? And have you ever thought of giving thanks for something as seemingly ordinary as your skin? If not, then now might be a good time. One square centimetre of your skin contains about 6 million cells, 100 sweat glands and 5,000 sensory corpuscles—as well as 200 pain points, 25 pressure points, 12 cold-sensitive points and 2 heat-sensitive points.[4] We take for granted this amazing part of our created bodies—but when we begin to investigate it, we are led through the gates of thanksgiving into the courts of praise. We join with the psalmist in crying out,

> I praise you because I am fearfully and won-
>     derfully made;
>   your works are wonderful,
>   I know that full well (Psalm 139:14).

Next, move on to your family and friends. Think about your social circles—how God skilfully wove them together, bringing people into your world for whom you will be ever grateful to share life with. For those with the eyes to see, the depths of His providence are swirling all around us. As a personal example, we've been married for seven years—and looking back, we're so appreciative of the depths of God's providence at work in our relationship. We first set eyes upon each other in a church car park in England. What a romantic, yet holy, setting! We praise God for that brief moment—that in His beautiful way He would let our paths cross for a short while, smiling upon the long-term plan He had to knit our lives together. Over the years, though we were living three hours apart, a strong friendship started to grow; and a while later we were both on the staff of a church, working with each other. In the end, it took a runaway mouse in the church building to bring us together. (It's a long story, but you'd be surprised what two hours of trying to catch a mouse together can do for a relationship!) The point is this: We must learn to rehearse the stories of God's providence in our lives—thanking Him for both the smallest details and the grandest designs. Every day God is working out His wonders all around us.

If we can begin to take regular, small steps into thankfulness, then before long we will pick up our pace and find ourselves taking great big strides of praise. Too often we neglect even the small things—for instance, saying grace before a meal. In one way, this is a small thing. Yet if we begin to adopt this discipline, we begin to carve out space two or three times each day to thank God for His provision. The arrival of the food on our table gives many reasons to be thankful. To illustrate this, let's consider the vegetables we eat. On the journey between the soil and our plates, they have been grown, harvested, cleaned, transported, sold and cooked. We thank God for their provision, but we must also thank Him for the many hands that have laboured to bring them to us.

Before long, we're on to big steps in thanksgiving—thanking God for some of the grand themes of the Christian life. The writer of Psalm 103 exhorts us to

> forget not all his benefits—
> who forgives all your sins
> and heals all your diseases,
> who redeems your life from the pit
> and crowns you with love and com-
> passion,
> who satisfies your desires with good things
> so that your youth is renewed like
> the eagle's (vv. 2-5).

Salvation, healing, forgiveness, compassion and renewal—these are themes we should visit every day of our walk with God, and each of them can be found at the place of the Cross. The hymn writer Fanny Crosby wrote, "Keep me near the cross," which is a great heart cry for any worshipper.[5] For when we stop going by the Cross, we begin to lose sight of the depths of the pit we've been rescued from—and the heights of the mercy that saved us.

A thankful heart may not come easily—we can be so quick to let something not going very well in our lives cloud over the multitude of little blessings we have to be grateful for. Or else we spend hours asking God for something, yet only minutes thanking Him when He answers our prayers. Another pitfall in worship is to spend lots of time telling God what we have done for Him and to neglect to thank Him for the far-more-momentous area of what He has done for us. In all of these areas, we must ask the Holy Spirit to help us cultivate a lifestyle and a mind-set of gratitude.

Another way to start out along this road is to thank Him as the God of yesterday, today and forever—the One who was and is and is to come. In other words, begin by recalling a wonder He has worked somewhere along your life's journey. Walk through your testimony in your heart and mind; go again by the place of the Cross and see all that He has won for you and done for you in that momentous place. Move on to the empty tomb and dwell for a moment on the joy of sharing in His resurrection. This is the first stage—thanking Him as the *God of yesterday*.

Next, bring gratitude for a kindness that He's worked in your life today—perhaps an answered prayer or a friendship you value. This is to worship Him as the *God of today*. And last, look to the horizon and thank Him in advance for a wonder still to come, praising Him as the *God of forever* and thanking Him for the life that is to come. This kind of model frees us up from a mentality of grumbling and trains us in the way of gratitude. We join with the hymn "Great Is Thy Faithfulness," reminding ourselves of God's consistent love and care for us in days gone by and worshipping Him as the bringer of "strength for today and bright hope for tomorrow."[6]

Mature worshippers of Jesus learn to bring an offering in every season of the soul, for every high and every low, knowing that the worth of Jesus outweighs each and every pain and pleasure in this life. Centred on Christ, wholesome worship has room both for the heights of joy and the pits of despair. Every blessing He pours out, we turn back to praise. And even when the dark times close in on us, still we will be singing out, "Blessed be Your name."

—〰—

OH THAT GOD WOULD BRING

US TO THE PLACE THAT EVEN WHEN

THE FAMILIAR AND THE

COMFORTABLE FALL AWAY BENEATH

US, STILL WE ARE FOUND WITH

AN UNDYING SONG OF

TRUST FLOWING FROM OUR LIPS

AND FROM OUR LIVES.

—〰—

## CHAPTER FIVE

# You Give and Take Away

The last section of the song "Blessed Be Your Name" comes straight from the story of Job. In what has to be one of the most intense stories in the whole of Scripture, Job is stripped of everything precious to him and suffers much hardship. Toward the beginning of his ordeal, he finds a way to the place of praise, falling to the ground in worship and crying out,

"The LORD gave and the LORD has taken away. Blessed be the name of the LORD" (Job 1:21, *NASB*).

This resounding line is a challenge for every worshipper. A call to trust deeply in the sovereignty of God, shaping our lives based not on the temporary things of the earth but on the eternal King of heaven. For devotion to stand the test of time and endure through every season of the soul, it cannot be based on the ever-changing circumstances of our lives—it must have its foundation on the never-changing worth of God.

In 1744, the hymn writer Charles Wesley was leading a worship gathering in an upstairs room in the city of Leeds, England. The meeting room was crammed full—when all of a sudden, the floor gave way, with all 100 people falling into the room below! Wesley's reaction to this situation was inspiring. Seeing first that no one was seriously injured, he began to sing the doxology: "Praise God from whom all blessings flow." Not only that, but afterward he composed several hymns based on this event—using the broken floor as a picture of the uncertain things of this world, and contrasting it with the unshakable nature of God, His Kingdom and His Word.

The question for us is this: What do *we* do when our world falls in? What shape does our worship take when things that we depend on give way beneath us?

Can we, as Wesley, be found with an unswerving song of worship on our lips? Oh that God would bring us to that place—that even when the familiar and the comfortable fall away beneath us, still we are found with an undying song of trust flowing from our lips and from our lives.

There may actually be times when trust is just about all we can bring as an offering to God. Times of pain and struggle, when we've come to the end of ourselves and feel like we have nothing left to give. In these moments, to say to God, "I trust You," can be an offering pleasing enough in and of itself. We trust that God cares for us with a deep Fatherly affection. We trust that His arm is never too short to save. We trust that He hears those who call upon His name. We trust that He is high enough to see things that we could never see. We trust that He is quick to show compassion, slow to anger and abounding in love. In all of these offerings, we are telling God that despite our circumstances, we still believe He is who He says He is. And God loves that kind of heart response.

As we mentioned in the introduction, since writing the song "Blessed Be Your Name," we've had the privilege of hearing so many testimonies of how worshippers have found a way to endure even in the harshest of life circumstances. Many of these testimonies have been beautiful and profound.[1]

Dunblane, Perthshire
19th June 2003

Dear Matt and Beth,

Our precious youngest daughter, Rachel, died on 25th February this year. She was 4 years old. We have 4 other children: 2 girls—Brodie, 18, and Maggie, 17; and 2 boys—Harry, 10, and William, 8. Rachel was a beautiful gift, loved by us more than I can begin to describe.

She was a totally healthy child until she took chicken pox in December 2002. It turned into pneumonitis, a rare complication, and she was rushed to intensive care in the Edinburgh kids' hospital, where she was on life support for nearly 3 weeks. She was very sick but made a wonderful recovery—delighting the doctors and nurses.

We brought her home on Christmas Eve, and although Rachel was very weak, we managed. It will always be our most memorable Christmas. She regained strength gradually and started to walk again after a few weeks, returning to her school nursery—full of joy in her recovery and very aware of how loved and special she was.

Then she became suddenly ill through the night of 24th February, and I rushed her to Stirling Royal Infirmary. She had developed septicaemia, which led to heart failure—and she died within 4 hours of reaching hospital. It is still hard for me to believe however often I have painfully relived the events of that day.

We are all Christians, and when we were thinking of Rachel's funeral, we all knew immediately that we wanted the song "Blessed Be Your Name" in the service. It had been sung in our church and was prominent when Rachel and I were in hospital, but it took on a strong significance for us after her death. The words gave us strength and said what we wanted to say.

There were about 400 people in Dunblane Cathedral for the funeral. Our pastor took the service, and God gave us the strength we prayed for. The band led "Blessed Be Your Name." It was beautiful, powerful and moving—and our family sang from our hearts.

Rachel will always be a part of us, and as time passes, it means such a lot when others remember her. We are missing her so much. The many tears I have shed while writing this letter have been strangely comforting amidst the pain. I have struggled very often to praise God since Rachel's funeral, but He does not let me go; and in the darkness, the only light and hope come from Christ, whose loving arms hold my darling Rachel.

With love,
From Ruth McColl

Columbus, Ohio, U.S.A.
4 April 2005

Dear Matt and Beth,

We lost our eighteen-year-old daughter, Natalie, two years ago in an auto accident. It was her last day of high school. Ten short days before her high school graduation. She was the light of our lives. My love for Jesus has helped me through some of my darkest times. When I became an active Christian, the only thing I ever asked of God was to please not test my love for Him through Natalie. I prayed that every day for eight years. At the hospital I kept telling all the pastors, "But this was the only thing I have ever truly asked of God."

It took me a few months to start attending church again. I wasn't mad at Him—I was hurt, confused and even scared of Him. It was and is so bittersweet. We prayed and prayed for a miracle that day. We watched all her young friends, sitting in the waiting room in prayer circles and asking for that miracle, but it was not to be.

To attend church services and sing praise to Him about all the miracles He has performed and about what a loving God He is and to not have my Natalie sitting next to me was so very hard.

Then we heard your song, and to us it just fit our situation so well that we now call it Natalie's song. Jeff and I always end up in tears when we get to the part about "He gives and takes away." That is so true. As a Christian, I understand that we are all God's children, big and small, young and old; but as a mother, she was my little girl. It is so hard to let go of her.

She was a hero to the end. She was an organ donor and saved four lives. She was always our "little special," but now she is to many, many more.

Blessings to you and your family.

With God's love,
Kathy Sayre

These worship-filled letters were written by worshippers who did not deny the pain of their loss, but stood in the midst of it, choosing to trust God. Heaven knows they have made a good choice.

Our pastor recently commented that Christ-centred funerals are some of the best showcases for Christianity. That for those who trust their lives to Jesus, there is a wonderful distinctive when it comes to marking loss. Outside of Christ, many a memorial service or funeral is a groping in the dark—a heavy cloud of grief with no clarity as to what lies beyond it. There may be a meaningful celebration of a person's days on the earth, but without a Christ-centred hope, this will always be outweighed by the lack of confidence in a life everlasting. When the world only brings a vocabulary of sorrow and loss, in contrast the memorial service of a worshipper of Jesus is infused with a deep sense of thankfulness and hope. Yes, there is still the pain of loss, but it's outweighed by what we know to be true of God and of His promises for those who love Him. Only those who are rooted in such a faith can dare to say, "The Lord gives and the Lord takes away. Blessed be the name of the Lord." Without a deep knowledge of the Father heart of God and a faith in His sovereign power and wisdom, it's far too dangerous a thing to pray.

One man who adopted this heart stance was the eighteenth-century English poet and hymn writer William Cowper. One of his most well-known hymns is an amazing poetic and biblical response that comes from a man surrendered to the sovereignty of God:

God moves in a mysterious way,
His wonders to perform;

He plants His footsteps in the sea
And rides upon the storm.

Deep in unfathomable mines
Of never-failing skill
He treasures up His bright designs
And works His sovereign will.

His purposes will ripen fast,
Unfolding every hour;
The bud may have a bitter taste,
But sweet will be the flower.

Blind unbelief is sure to err
And scan His work in vain;
God is His own interpreter,
And He will make it plain.[2]

What an incredible expression of worship from a
heart assured that we can trust our lives fully to God!
Cowper worshipped Him as the One with all things
under His control—that even when he could not fathom God's ways in his life, God was working out His
good, pleasing and perfect will. The hymn declares,
"God is His own interpreter." In other words, we can-

not always speak for Him or figure Him out. In His own timing, we will begin to perceive the wonders that He is performing.

But the most amazing thing of all about this hymn is that Cowper suffered with manic depression—something that he'd been plagued by for many years and that doctors in his day had little comprehension of. How incredible that he could write such a powerful hymn wrapped around the theme of the sovereignty of God, while living day by day under such a dark cloud! In fact, the day after writing this hymn, Cowper sunk into a deep depression—and for the rest of his days on the earth, he never really recovered. That, in itself, is a mystery.

Yes, there are some things we will never understand while we walk upon this earth. There comes a time when we simply have to submit to the mystery. Why do the young sometimes lose their lives so early on? Why can some people who are so good with children never have sons and daughters of their own? Why would a tsunami hit so hard to wipe out hundreds of thousands of lives in an instant? Theologians and philosophers can weigh in with some interesting and, at times, convincing arguments. But for those who are in the midst of such circumstances, these cerebral answers, feed the mind or offer some explanation as they might, may never fully serve to calm the soul. Sometimes, as we stand there in the midst of our pain and confusion, all we can do is submit to the mystery—knowing that He who gives and takes away is infinitely wiser and more loving than we could ever fathom.

And even if our earthly days cannot make sense of some of these experiences, then our days in heaven surely will. To those who are in Christ, ultimately everything will make sense. The writer of Romans describes it like this:

> I consider that our present sufferings are not worth comparing with the glory that will be revealed in us (8:18).

We stand on the unshakable hope of all that is to come—for our present suffering, as real and as awful as it may be, will be nothing in comparison with the glory that will be revealed in us. As the apostle Paul encourages us,

> Therefore we do not lose heart. Though outwardly we are wasting away, yet inwardly we are being renewed day by day. For our light and

momentary troubles are achieving for us an
eternal glory that far outweighs them all. So
we fix our eyes not on what is seen, but on
what is unseen. For what is seen is temporary,
but what is unseen is eternal (2 Corinthians
4:16-18).

Somehow, this pain, which thunders violently in
the very cores of our beings, will be but a mere whis-
per when compared with the radiance and satisfac-
tion to one day be bestowed upon us. It's good news
from a distant land, the glimmering haze of a bright
hope to come. And yet it is not escapism—for though
this hope will be fully unveiled to us on that day, even
now we can live in Christ, and He in us. We walk on:
sorrowful, yet always rejoicing; perplexed, but never
in despair; at times having nothing, and yet possess-
ing everything.

The road to our final destination will indeed be
marked with suffering. Jesus is looking for worshippers who will choose Him even in the midst of their
pain. A people with a cry of "Blessed be Your name"
resonating in the depths of their souls. And no matter how painful life becomes, He will surely be worth
the struggle.

# Blessed Be Your Name

Blessed be Your name in the land that is plentiful,
Where Your streams of abundance flow,
Blessed be Your name.
And blessed be Your name when I'm found in the desert place,
Though I walk through the wilderness,
Blessed be Your name.

Every blessing You pour out I'll turn back to praise.
And when the darkness closes in, Lord,
Still I will say,

Blessed be the name of the Lord,
Blessed be Your name.
Blessed be the name of the Lord,
Blessed be Your glorious name.

Blessed be Your name when the sun's shining down on me,
When the world's "all as it should be,"
Blessed be Your name.

And blessed be Your name on the road marked with suffering,
Though there's pain in the offering,
Blessed be Your name.

Every blessing You pour out I'll turn back to praise,
And when the darkness closes in, Lord,
Still I will say,

Blessed be the name of the Lord,
Blessed be Your name.
Blessed be the name of the Lord,
Blessed be Your glorious name.

You give and take away,
You give and take away,
My heart will choose to say,
"Lord, blessed be Your name."

—∿—

# Acknowledgments

Thanks to

Don Williams and Louie Giglio for support

and feedback;

Claire Prosser and Ellie Redman, for lots of

research and support;

Andrew Philip and Andy Hutch, for artistic endeavour;

Jo Trevor, for the statistics;

Pastor Jack Hayford, for your wise opening words

to the American edition,

and Andy Hickford to the British edition;

all at Regal Books in the U.S.

and Hodder and Stoughton in the U.K.

—∿—

# Bible References Contained in This Book

The following is a complete list of all the Bible verses referenced in this book. We hope the verses will propel you to further study, and to worship.

## Chapter 1

I remember it all—oh, how well I remember—the feeling of hitting the bottom. But there's one other thing I remember, and remembering, I keep a grip on hope: GOD's loyal love couldn't have run out, his merciful love couldn't have dried up. They're created new every morning.

How great your faithfulness!
Lamentations 3:20-23, *THE MESSAGE*


How long, O LORD? Will you forget me forever?
    How long will you hide your face from me?
How long must I wrestle with my thoughts
    and every day have sorrow in my heart?
How long will my enemy triumph over me?

But I trust in your unfailing love;
    my heart rejoices in your salvation.
I will sing to the Lord,
    for he has been good to me.
Psalm 13:1-2,5-6


Why are you downcast, O my soul?
    Why so disturbed within me?
Put your hope in God,
    for I will yet praise him,
    my Saviour and my God.
Psalm 42:5-6,11


## Chapter 2

If one part suffers, every part suffers with it;
if one part is honoured, every part rejoices
with it.
1 Corinthians 12:26

My God, my God, why have you forsaken me?
Psalm 22:1; Mark 15:33

"If we are thrown into the blazing furnace, the God we serve is able to save us from it, and he will rescue us from your hand, O king. But even if he does not, we want you to know, O king, that we will not serve your gods or worship the image of gold you have set up."
Daniel 3:17-18

But as for me, I came so close to the edge of
    the cliff!
    My feet were slipping, and I was almost
        gone.
For I envied the proud
    when I saw them prosper despite their
        wickedness.
They seem to live such a painless life;
    their bodies are so healthy and strong.
They aren't troubled like other people
    or plagued with problems like everyone
        else.
Was it for nothing that I kept my heart pure
    and kept myself from doing wrong?

I must have seemed like a senseless animal
> to you.
Yet I still belong to you;
> you are holding my right hand.
You will keep on guiding me with your
> counsel,
> leading me to a glorious destiny.
Whom have I in heaven but you?
> I desire you more than anything on
> earth.
My health may fail, and my spirit may grow
> weak,
> but God remains the strength of my heart;
> he is mine forever.

Psalm 73:2-5,13,22-26, *NLT*


Be joyful always; pray continually; give thanks
in all circumstances, for this is God's will for
you in Christ Jesus.

1 Thessalonians 5:16-18


Sorrowful, yet always rejoicing; poor, yet making many rich; having nothing, and yet pos-
sessing everything.

2 Corinthians 6:10

## Chapter 3

Give thanks in all circumstances, for this is God's will for you in Christ Jesus.

1 Thessalonians 5:18

Consider it pure joy, my brothers, whenever you face trials of many kinds, because you know that the testing of your faith develops perseverance. Perseverance must finish its work so that you may be mature and complete, not lacking anything.

James 1:2-4

In this you greatly rejoice, though now for a little while you may have had to suffer grief in all kinds of trials. These have come so that your faith—of greater worth than gold, which perishes even though refined by fire— may be proved genuine and may result in praise, glory and honour when Jesus Christ is revealed.

1 Peter 1:6-7

That is why, for Christ's sake, I delight in weaknesses, in insults, in hardships, in persecutions, in difficulties. For when I am weak, then I am strong.

2 Corinthians 12:10

Endure hardship as discipline; God is treating you as sons. For what son is not disciplined by his father? If you are not disciplined (and everyone undergoes discipline), then you are illegitimate children and not true sons. Our fathers disciplined us for a little while as they thought best; but God disciplines us for our good, that we may share in his holiness. No discipline seems pleasant at the time, but painful. Later on, however, it produces a harvest of righteousness and peace for those who have been trained by it.

Hebrews 12:7-8,10-11

And it was only right that God—who made everything and for whom everything was made—should bring his many children into glory. Through the suffering of Jesus, God made him a perfect leader, one fit to bring them into their salvation.

Hebrews 2:10, *NLT*

Therefore, there is now no condemnation for those who are in Christ Jesus.

Romans 8:1

"You intended to harm me, but God intended it for good to accomplish what is now being done, the saving of many lives."

Genesis 50:20

The second son he named Ephraim and said, "It is because God has made me fruitful in the land of my suffering."

Genesis 41:52

"He cuts off every branch in me that bears no fruit, while every branch that does bear fruit he prunes so that it will be even more fruitful."

John 15:2

## Chapter 4

Enter his gates with thanksgiving
and his courts with praise;
give thanks to him and praise his name.

Psalm 100:4-5

I praise you because I am fearfully and won-
   derfully made;
   your works are wonderful,
   I know that full well.

Psalm 139:14

Praise the Lord, O my soul,
   and forget not all his benefits—
who forgives all your sins
   and heals all your diseases,
who redeems your life from the pit
   and crowns you with love and compassion,
who satisfies your desires with good things
   so that your youth is renewed like the
      eagle's.

Psalm 103:2-5

## Chapter 5

"The LORD gave and the LORD has taken
away. Blessed be the name of the LORD."

Job 1:21, *NASB*

I consider that our present sufferings are not
worth comparing with the glory that will be
revealed in us.

Romans 8:18

Therefore we do not lose heart. Though outwardly we are wasting away, yet inwardly we are being renewed day by day. For our light and momentary troubles are achieving for us an eternal glory that far outweighs them all. So we fix our eyes not on what is seen, but on what is unseen. For what is seen is temporary, but what is unseen is eternal.

2 Corinthians 4:16-18

—∿—

# Recommended Reading on Suffering

Carson, D. A. *How Long, O Lord?: Reflections on Suffering and Evil.* Grand Rapids, MI: Baker Book House, 1990.

Lewis, C. S. *The Problem of Pain.* San Francisco: HarperSanFrancisco, 2001.

Yancey, Philip. *Where Is God When It Hurts?* Grand Rapids, MI: Zondervan, 1997.

—∿—

# Endnotes

**Chapter 1**

1. Edward Mote, "The Solid Rock," quoted in *The Celebration Hymnal* (n.p.: Word Music and Integrity Music, 1997), song no. 526.
2. Anonymous, quoted in David Pytches, *Can Anyone Be a Leader?* (Trowbridge, UK: Eagle Publishing, 2004), p. 43.

**Chapter 2**

1. Excerpted from "Whom Have I But You" by David Ruis. © 1996 Mercy/Vineyard Publishing (ASCAP)/Vineyard Songs (Canada). Admin. by Vineyard Music Global worldwide.
2. John Newton, "Amazing Grace," quoted in *The Celebration Hymnal* (n.p.: Word Music and Integrity Music, 1997), song no. 343.
3. Eugene Peterson, *The Message of David* (London: Marshall Pickering, 1997), n.p.
4. Frederick W. Schmidt, Jr., *When Suffering Persists* (Harrisburg, PA: Morehouse Publishing, 2001), p. 26.
5. Mark Greene, lecture at a songwriters' consultation, UK, November 2004.
6. Ibid.
7. Schmidt, Jr., *When Suffering Persists,* p. 28.
8. Tim Hughes, "When the Tears Fall," © 2003 Thankyou Music/Adm. by worshiptogether.com songs. Excl. UK &

Europe, adm. by Kingsway Music: tym@kingsway.co.uk. Used by pemission.

9. Laurence Tuttiett, "Father, Let Me Dedicate," 1864. In the original, the first line uses "year" instead of "life."

10. John Piper, *Pierced by the Word* (Sisters, OR: Multnomah Publishers, 2003), p. 40.

### Chapter 3

1. "Mental Health," *World Health Organization,* 2005. http://www.who.int/mental_health/en/ (accessed May 4, 2005).

2. "Africa Fact Sheet," *UNAIDS,* April 3, 2005. http://www.unaids.org/EN/media/fact+sheets.asp (accessed May 4, 2005).

3. C. S. Lewis, quoted in Russell Stannard, *Why?: Why Evil? Why Suffering? Why Death?* (Oxford: Lion Publishing, 2003), p. 82.

4. C. S. Lewis, *The Problem of Pain* (San Francisco: HarperSanFrancisco, 2001), n.p.

5. Madame Jeanne Marie de la Mothe Guyon, quoted in *NIV Worship Bible* (Grand Rapids, MI: Zondervan Publishing House, 2000), p. 59.

6. Frederick W. Schmidt, Jr., *When Suffering Persists* (Harrisburg, PA: Morehouse Publishing, 2001), p. 23.

7. Oswald Chambers, *My Utmost for His Highest* (New York: Dodd, Mead and Company, 1935), reading for October 11.

### Chapter 4

1. Alfred Painter, quoted in "Alfred Painter," *Wisdom Quotes,* 2004. http://www.wisdomquotes.com/002828.html (accessed May 11, 2005).

2. Wernet Gitt, *The Wonder of Man,* trans. Jaap Kies and Carl Wieland (Bielefield, Germany: Christliche Literatur-Verbreitung, 1999), n.p.

3. Ibid.
4. Ibid.
5. Fanny Crosby, "Near the Cross," quoted in *The Celebration Hymnal* (n.p.: Word Music and Integrity Music, 1997), song no. 319.
6. Thomas O. Chrisholm, "Great Is Thy Faithfulness," © 1923 renewed 1951 Hope Publishing Company. Administered by Copy Care, P. O. Box 77, Hailsham BN27 3EF, UK. Used by permission.

**Chapter 5**
1. These letters have been printed with the permission of the writers, Ruth McColl and Kathy Sayre.
2. William Cowper, "God Moves in a Mysterious Way," 1774.

For more worship resources
from Matt Redman, visit